532

Camdean School

WORKING WITH WATER

Neil Ardley

Series consultant: Professor Eric Laithwaite

Franklin Watts

London   New York   Toronto   Sydney

The author
Neil Ardley gained a degree in science and worked as
a research chemist and patent agent before entering
publishing. He is now a full-time writer and is the
author of more than fifty information books on
science, natural history and music.

The consultant
Eric Laithwaite is Professor of Heavy Electrical
Engineering at Imperial College, London. A well-
known television personality and broadcaster, he is
best known for his inventions on linear motors.

© 1983 Franklin Watts Ltd
First published in Great
Britain in 1983
by Franklin Watts Ltd
12a Golden Square
London W1

Reprinted 1983

First published in the United
States of America by
Franklin Watts Inc.
387 Park Avenue South
New York
N.Y. 10016

Printed in Belgium

UK edition:
ISBN 0 86313 021 6
US edition:
ISBN 0-531-04519-6
Library of Congress
Catalog Card Number:
82-51008

Designed by
David Jefferis

Illustrated by Janos Marffy,
Hayward Art Group and
Arthur Tims

ACTION SCIENCE

WORKING WITH WATER

Contents

Equipment

You will need the following equipment to carry out all the activities in this book.

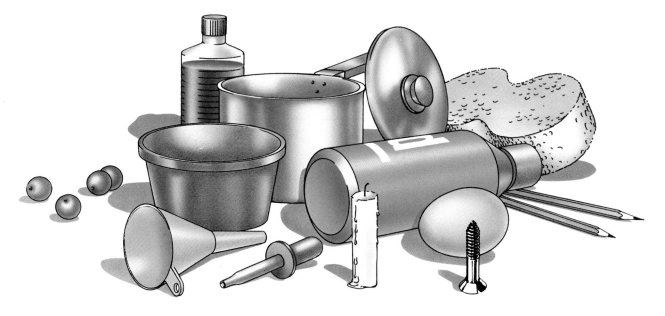

Clear plastic tube at least 30 cm (12 in) long
Funnel
Dropper
Two bowls (a sink will do for one)
Two jars or glasses
Stiff dry sponge
Board
Pencil
Plastic film or plastic bag
Saucepan and lid
Spring balance
Large stone
Egg and salt

Plasticine or modelling clay
Methylated spirits
Empty detergent bottle
Coins
Washing-up liquid
Needle
Tweezers
Handkerchief
Cooking oil
Syrup
Cork
Grapes
Candle
Screw-top jar

Introduction

Water is a fluid, which means that it flows. It is one of two great fluids on Earth. The other one is air and, like air, water plays an important part in our lives. It not only supports life but controls the weather, helps to shape the land, enables us to clean things, allows us to travel by boat, gives us fun and exercise in swimming and so on. All this is possible because of the various ways in which water behaves.

By doing the activities with water in this book, you will find out how water behaves and how it can do unusual things, like flowing uphill and disappearing into thin air. You'll also understand why water acts as it does—why it is easier to swim in the sea than a lake and why some insects can walk on water, for example. You can also have some fun with water; you can make an egg float and empty a container of water without touching it, to mention just two tricks that you can try.

✳ This symbol is used throughout the book. It shows you where to find the scientific explanation for the results of the experiment.

Water level

Water always finds its own level. This is why it flows into holes and out of taps.

Getting level

Take a funnel and place it in one end of a long clear plastic tube. Hold both ends of the tube in one hand and pour some water into the funnel with the other. Watch how the water flows through the tube until it reaches the same level on each side. Raise or lower one side of the tube. The water always moves to the same level on each side whatever you do.

✳ Water finds its own level because it tries to get as low down as possible. When you dig a hole in a beach, it often fills with water. Water from the sea comes through the sand and fills the hole to sea level.

water level

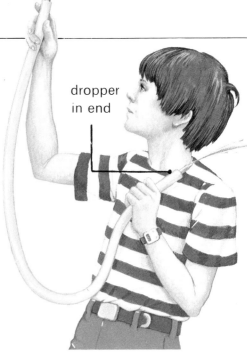

dropper
in end

Make a fountain

With the funnel, fill the tube almost to the top. Then pinch the open end of the tube between your fingers or place a dropper into it. Now lower this end beneath the water level in the tube. The water spurts from the tube like a fountain. By lowering this end, you can make the fountain spurt higher. But notice how the jet only rises to almost the same height as the water level in the tube. This is because the water is still trying to reach the same level.

△ Some fountains are fed with water from a high lake and work like this experiment. Others have pumps to produce a jet.

water tank
in roof

pipe feeds
bath tap

✳ Water taps in kitchens and bathrooms work in the same way. The water comes from a high tank either in the roof or outside the building. When a tap is opened, the water flows down through the pipes to reach the lowest level.

Raising water

Use the air to make water rise and move.

Fill a glass upside-down

Place a glass in water, turn it upside-down and lift it slowly. Watch what happens when the bottom of the glass rises above the surface of the water. The water stays in the glass and is raised with it. But as the top of the glass breaks the surface, all the water falls out of the glass.

※ Air presses down on the water, pushing water up into the glass. But when the top of the glass breaks the surface, air can rush into it instead. The air no longer supports the water, so the water falls out.

air   air

△ Air pressure pushes water up into the glass. The same happens when you drink with a straw.

Make a siphon

Fill a tube with water, placing a finger over the bottom end. Put this end under some water in a bowl, and place the other end in a lower bowl. Take away your finger and see how the water flows up the tube and down into the lower bowl.

✳ This is a siphon. It works because air pressure pushes the water up the tube and around the bend. After that, the water continues to flow because it tries to reach the same level in both bowls.

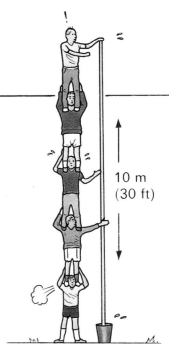

10 m (30 ft)

△ Air pressure is strong enough to push water about 10 metres (30 feet) up a tube.

Make sure this bowl is higher than the other one.

Water can push

What does water do when things enter it?

△ Before you do this trick, make sure that the jar is big enough and the water is deep enough to get your thumb or fingers well into the water.

The watery see-saw trick

Take a slim piece of board and balance it on a pencil. Place two jars of water on the board like a see-saw. Tell your friends that you can make the see-saw tip without touching either the jars or the board. To do this, you lower your thumb or several fingers into the water in the higher jar without touching the sides.

✴ This trick works because as you lower your thumb or fingers into the water, they push the water aside and the water rises in level. This is the same as adding water to the jar. The jar gets heavier and therefore tips the see-saw over.

10

Feel the force of water

Take a large sheet of thin plastic film or a plastic bag and wrap it tightly around your hand and wrist. Now dip your arm into a deep bowl of water. Feel how strongly the water pushes on your hand as you lower it deeper into the water.

△ Hold the plastic tightly around your wrist as you plunge your hand into the water. The water compresses the plastic so that you can feel the water pushing.

※ As anything goes under water, some water is pushed aside, making the water rise in level. This water pushes down and against the object. It pushes against your hand just as it pushes against any object in the water. As more of the object enters the water, more water rises and the push becomes greater.

Floating and sinking

Why do some things float on water and others sink in water?

Will it float?

Find several objects made of different materials. They must be solid and not hollow. First guess which will float and which will sink, and then place them in a bowl of water to find out. Some large and heavy objects like apples float, while small light objects like pins may sink.

✳ The push of the water tries to support a solid object. But if the object weighs more than this push, it sinks. This happens *only* if the object is made of a material like metal that has a greater density than water. If the density of the material is less than that of water, the object floats.

Lower the object beneath the water, but do not let it touch the bottom of the bowl.

Losing weight

Ask yourself or some friends how much things weigh in water. Then take a spring balance and a stone. Weigh the stone by suspending it from the balance. Now, without taking it off the balance, lower the stone into some water. See how much it weighs now. It is much less!

✴ The stone weighs less in water because of the push or support it gets from the water. This support is equal to the difference between the weight of the stone in air and its weight in the water. As the support is not enough to hold up the stone, the stone sinks.

△ The support that the stone gets from the water is equal to the weight of the water that the stone forces aside and upwards. The reason for this is that the same amount of water pushes down and back against the stone.

Afloat in a boat

Why is it that boats can float on water even though they are made of materials like metal that normally sink?

Make a boat
Take a metal saucepan lid. Carefully lower it flat on to the surface of some water in a bowl. It will float like a boat. Now pick up the lid and lower it upright into the water. Let go and it sinks.

△ For many centuries, people thought that boats could not be made of iron because they would sink. This experiment shows that an iron boat floats easily. Any object that is hollow like a boat will float. The air inside a hollow object gives the whole object a density that is less than that of water, so it floats.

✳ As the lid enters the water, it pushes aside some water and the water pushes back. When it is lowered flat, the broad shape of the lid pushes aside a lot of water —enough water to push back and support the lid so that it floats. Steel boats float for this reason. When the lid is lowered upright, it is narrow where it enters the water. It does not push aside enough water to hold it up, so it sinks.

14

Make a sponge both float and sink
Take a stiff, dry sponge and drop it on
some water in a bowl. It will float high
above the surface. Push it under the water
and squeeze the sponge. Now it will sink
beneath the surface.

✹ When the sponge is dry, it contains a
lot of air. This gives it a low density. When
the sponge is squeezed under water, the air
bubbles out and the sponge fills with
water. Its density is now slightly more than
the density of water, so it sinks below the
surface.

△ A sponge must be
stiff and dry in order to
float. If it is not, the
holes in the sponge fill
rapidly with water so
that no air remains
inside the sponge. This
makes it sink.

Differing densities

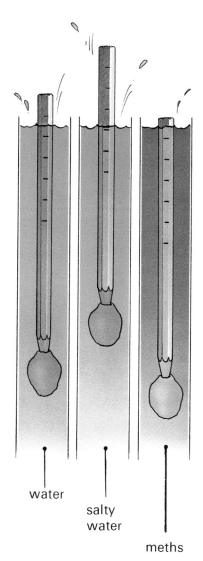

water

salty
water

meths

An object floats differently in different liquids, depending on their densities.

Make a hydrometer

Take a pencil and mark a scale along its length. Stick a small lump of plasticine or modelling clay to one end. Adjust the plasticine so that the pencil floats upright in water. See which mark on the scale is at the surface. Now float it in some salty water and some methylated spirits. See which marks are at the surface now. The pencil floats higher in salty water and lower in methylated spirits.

✳ This instrument is called a hydrometer. It measures the density of liquids. The greater the density of the liquid, the higher the hydrometer floats. Salty water therefore has a greater density than ordinary water, and methylated spirits has a smaller density. The support that the hydrometer gets from the liquid depends on the density of the liquid that it pushes aside. If the density of the liquid is greater, the amount of liquid pushed aside weighs more, and so the support is greater. The hydrometer is therefore pushed higher by the liquid.

16

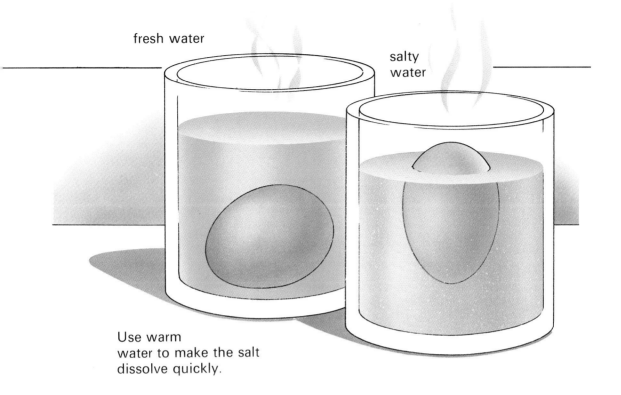

fresh water

salty water

Use warm water to make the salt dissolve quickly.

The floating egg trick

Show your friends that an egg sinks in water, then tell them that you can make it float. First prepare another glass of water in which you have dissolved some salt. Do this by stirring some table salt into the water. Then place the egg in the salty water and it will float!

✹ This trick works because salty water has a higher density than ordinary water. The egg has a density that is slightly greater than that of ordinary water but slightly less than the density of salty water. It therefore sinks in ordinary water but floats in salty water.

△ As salty water is more dense than fresh water, the amount of water pushed aside and upwards by the egg weighs more if the water is salty. It gives the egg more support and enables it to float. This is why it is easier to swim in the salty water of the sea than the fresh water of a lake or swimming pool.

Liquid layers

Make water float, sink and mix.

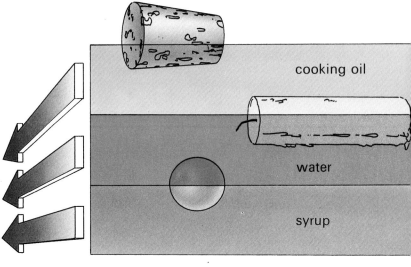

cooking oil

water

syrup

△ After pouring, the three liquids separate into layers. They do not mix because they have different densities. Oil has a smaller density than water and syrup has a greater density. All the liquids and the solid objects float at different levels in order of their density.

Floating in order

Take a glass and pour some syrup into it. Next pour some cooking oil on to the syrup and then add some water. The three liquids will form separate layers floating on one another. Now place a small grape, a piece of candle and piece of cork in the tumbler. The grape floats on the syrup, the candle on the water and the cork on the oil.

✳ The three liquids and the cork, candle and grape all have different densities. The lowest density goes to the top and the greatest density to the bottom.

18

Mix oil and water

Take a clean glass bottle or jar with a screw top. Pour in some water and some cooking oil. Screw the top on hard and shake the bottle to mix the oil and water. They always separate into layers, no matter how much you shake the bottle. Make them mix by adding a few drops of washing-up liquid and shaking again. As the foam clears, you should see a milky liquid instead of the two layers.

The oil and water mix because the washing-up liquid breaks the oil up into tiny droplets. These mix with the water to form an emulsion.

△ Oil and water do not mix.

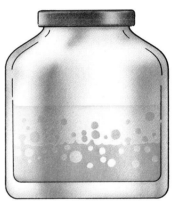

△ Even shaking does not mix them.

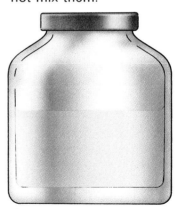

△ Add washing-up liquid and shake again.

Water pressure

Placing water under pressure can make it move quickly.

Jet power

Take an empty detergent bottle and remove the top. Fill the bottle with water and push the top back on. Now go outside and squeeze the bottle hard. See how far you can make a jet of water spurt from the bottle. Take the top off the bottle and try again. You will discover that the water does not go as far.

✳ As you squeeze the bottle, you place the water inside under pressure. It can only escape through the hole, making a jet. As you squeeze harder, the water pressure becomes greater, producing a bigger jet. But if the hole is wider, the pressure is less and the jet is smaller.

△ Like squeezing the bottle, a garden hose is fed with water under pressure to make the water spurt out in a jet.

20

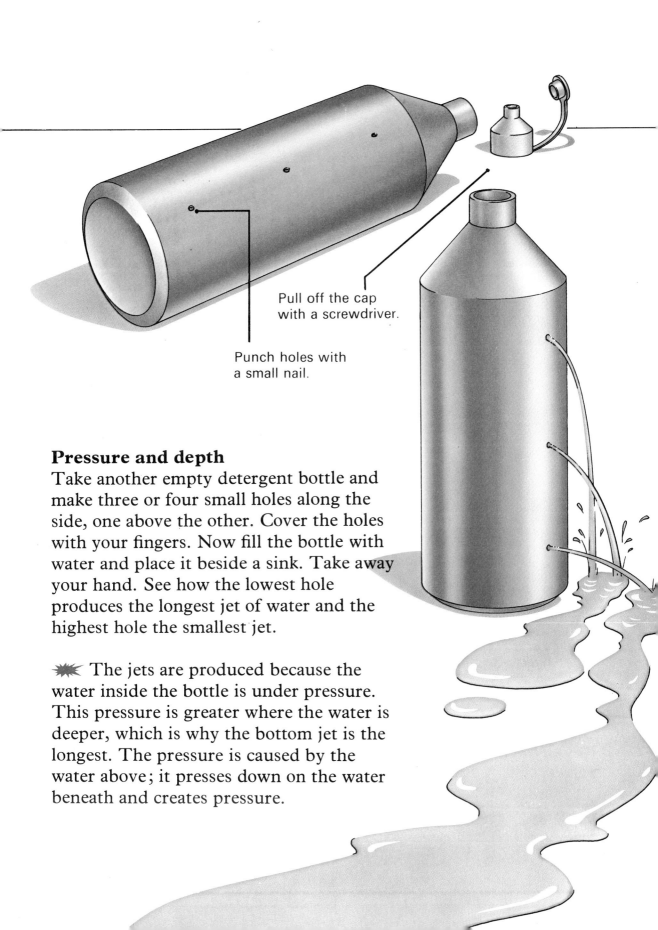

Pull off the cap
with a screwdriver.

Punch holes with
a small nail.

Pressure and depth

Take another empty detergent bottle and
make three or four small holes along the
side, one above the other. Cover the holes
with your fingers. Now fill the bottle with
water and place it beside a sink. Take away
your hand. See how the lowest hole
produces the longest jet of water and the
highest hole the smallest jet.

The jets are produced because the
water inside the bottle is under pressure.
This pressure is greater where the water is
deeper, which is why the bottom jet is the
longest. The pressure is caused by the
water above; it presses down on the water
beneath and creates pressure.

Water has skin

△ Hold each coin half in the water and then release it so that it slips gently into the water.

Test the strength of a water surface.

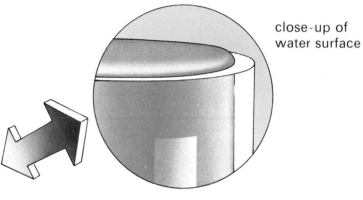

close-up of water surface

Curving water

Take a clean glass and fill it with water to the brim. See how many coins you can put in the glass before it overflows. You'll find that many more coins will go into the glass than you expected. See how the surface curves up above the rim of the glass. This is why the glass can take a lot of coins.

✳ The surface of the water curves because the top layer of the water forms an invisible skin over the water. This skin keeps the water from flowing over the edges until there are too many coins in the glass and the water breaks through the skin. The skin is caused by surface tension.

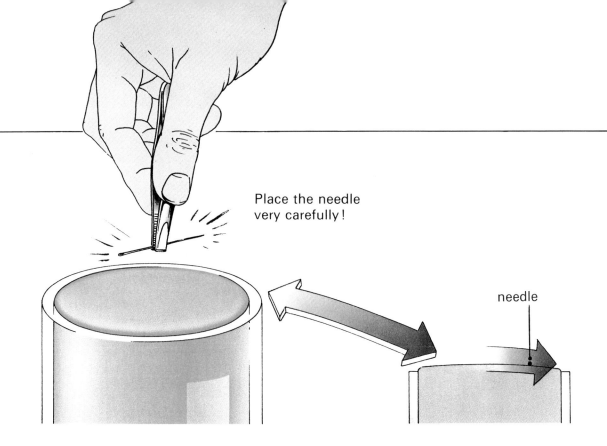

Place the needle
very carefully!

needle

Floating needles

Tell your friends that you can make metal float on water. To prove it, hold a needle in a pair of tweezers, gradually lower it on to the surface of the water and gently let it go. If you are very careful, the needle will float on the surface. Now tell them that you can make it sink without touching or moving the glass or the water. Let a drop of washing-up liquid fall into the water. The needle will sink immediately.

✳ The surface skin of the water holds the needle with enough force to support it. Adding detergent decreases the surface tension so that it can no longer support the needle and it sinks.

△ If the glass is full to the brim, the needle slides down the curve in the water surface.

▽ The pond skater is a water insect which is so light that it can walk on the surface skin of the water.

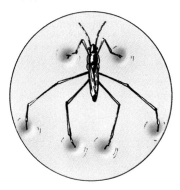

On the move

The force in a water surface is strong enough to produce movement.

Empty a bowl without trying
Make water go from one bowl to another without touching the bowl or the water. Take a clean handkerchief. Lower one corner into one bowl of water and place the opposite corner in another bowl. The water gradually spreads through the handkerchief, so that the lower bowl slowly fills with water.

△ Surface tension makes water rise through the fibres of the handkerchief in the upper bowl. It then flows through the handkerchief into the lower bowl.

Be patient. This takes time to work.

✳ Surface tension makes water rise of its own accord up very narrow tubes. The handkerchief contains many narrow spaces between the cotton fibres and the water moves through them. This is why a towel or a flannel easily soaks up water.

24

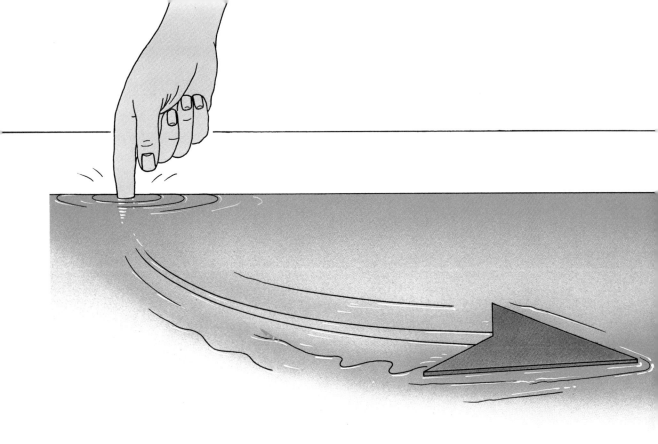

Paper speedboats

Make a paper speedboat as shown and float it. Now place a drop of washing-up liquid on one finger. Gently lower it into the water just behind the speedboat, and the boat will shoot forward as if by magic. This trick will only work once. To make it work again, you'll need fresh clean water.

✳ As the boat floats on the water, surface tension makes the skin of the water pull on it in all directions. It therefore does not move. But when the detergent enters the water, it decreases the surface tension behind the boat. The surface tension in front of the boat is now stronger and it immediately pulls the boat forward.

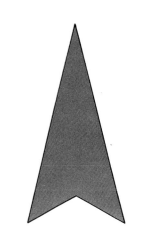

△ Make the speedboat by cutting a boat-like shape out of flat card or stiff paper.

Invisible water

Make water vanish into thin air and then make it appear from nowhere.

Vanishing water
Take a small glass and fill it with warm water to a mark on the side. Pour the water into a large saucer and fill the glass again to the same level. Place the saucer and the glass on a windowsill so that the Sun can shine on them, and open the window if it is not too cold. Then cover the glass by placing a large tumbler upside-down over it. See that the water in the saucer gradually decreases over a few hours and eventually disappears. The water in the glass does not fall in level at all.

✳ When water is open to the air, it evaporates. It forms invisible water vapour, which mixes with the air. The water continually forms more water vapour to take its place, and the water gradually all turns into water vapour and disappears. This is how washing dries when it is hung out on a line.

The large tumbler prevents all the water evaporating because it stops the water vapour escaping. The air inside becomes full of water vapour.

△ If it is windy, the air blows the water vapour away and the water evaporates faster. It also helps if the Sun warms the water. If it is not sunny, try using a portable lamp, placing the bulb near the water.

26

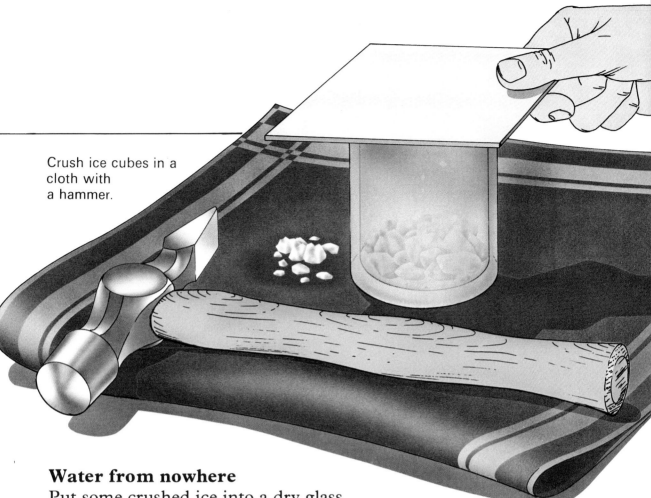

Crush ice cubes in a cloth with a hammer.

Water from nowhere

Put some crushed ice into a dry glass,
cover it with a card and wait a few minutes.
Gradually the side of the glass goes misty.
Run a finger around the glass: it is wet.
Where has the water come from?

✳ The water comes from invisible water
vapour in the air. Because the side of the
glass is cold, the water vapour condenses
on the glass. It changes into liquid water,
forming small drops of water and making
the glass misty.

Clouds are made of small drops of water
that condense from water vapour in the
cool air high above the ground.

△ This experiment will
not work if the air is
completely dry and
contains no water
vapour. This may
happen if it is very hot
or freezing cold outside.

Dew forms overnight
when water vapour
condenses on the cold
ground, just as droplets
form on the cold glass.

Making solutions

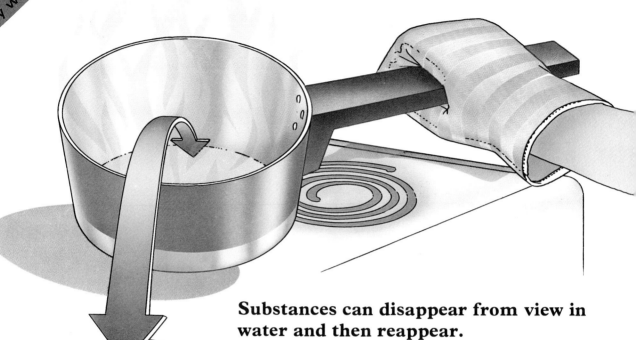

△ As in this experiment, much salt is made by letting pools of sea water evaporate to leave the salt behind.

Substances can disappear from view in water and then reappear.

Making salt

Stir some salt into water until the salt disappears. Dip a finger into the water and taste it: it is salty. Now put some of the salty clear water into a saucepan. Place the pan on a cooker and heat it. Notice that a white powder appears as the water boils away. Let the saucepan cool and taste the powder. The salt has reappeared.

The water dissolves the salt to form a solution of salt. Then when it is heated, only the water boils away. The salt does not and is left behind.

cloud

Purifying water

Repeat the same experiment, but this time place a lid on the saucepan. Before all the salty water boils away, carefully pick up the lid. Use a cloth to avoid being burned. You will see that drops of water have formed on the lid. When it is cool, taste the water. It is pure, not salty.

✳ This experiment shows that pure water boils away and that all the salt is left behind. The steam condenses on the lid to give drops of pure water. Rain water is pure water that has evaporated from the sea and other sources of water on land, and has then condensed to form raindrops in clouds.

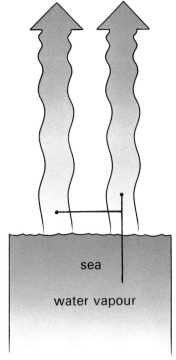

sea

water vapour

Pure water condenses on the inside of the lid.

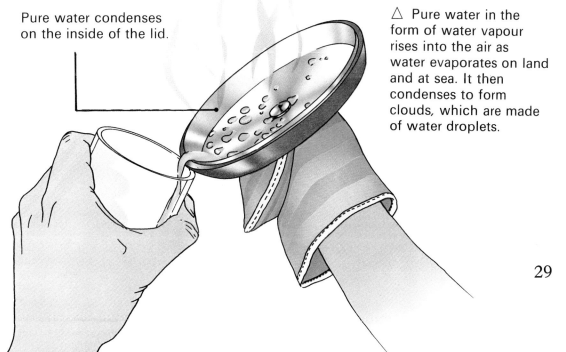

△ Pure water in the form of water vapour rises into the air as water evaporates on land and at sea. It then condenses to form clouds, which are made of water droplets.

29

Glossary

Condensation
Condensation happens when invisible water vapour in the air forms liquid water. The water molecules in the vapour normally stay apart. But if they are forced together, they form groups of molecules and liquid water is produced.

Density
The density of anything depends on how much a set amount of it weighs. A block of metal weighs more than a block of wood that is the same size. The metal therefore has a greater density than wood. If you could weigh a block of water of the same size, it would weigh less than the metal block but more than the wooden block. Metal therefore has a greater density than water, and wood has a lower density. This is why metal sinks and wood floats in water.

Emulsion
An emulsion is a mixture of two liquids that do not normally mix. An emulsifying agent like a detergent breaks one liquid up into tiny droplets that mix with the other liquid. Milk, cream, sauces and many paints are emulsions. Detergents clean because they make the grease that sticks dirt to crockery, cutlery and clothes mix with the washing water. The dirt comes away and mixes with the water. Soap cleans in the same way.

Evaporation
When water evaporates, some of it turns into water vapour. This happens because some of the water molecules at the surface of the water jump out of the water. They form water vapour, which mixes with the air. Water evaporates quickly if it is warm.

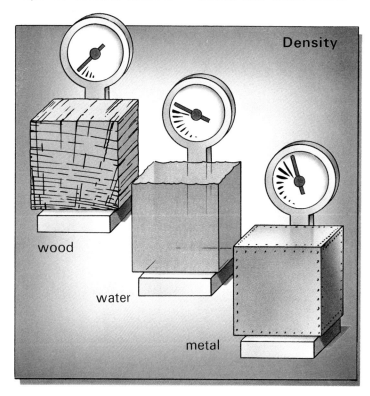

Density

wood

water

metal

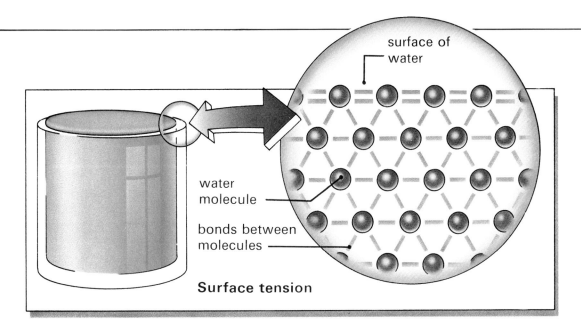

surface of
water

water
molecule

bonds between
molecules

Surface tension

Molecules
Molecules are tiny particles. They are so small that they cannot be seen even under powerful microscopes. A drop of water contains millions upon millions of water molecules. Everything has its own kind of molecules. Water consists of water molecules, air contains air molecules, sugar is made of sugar molecules and so on.

Solution
When a material like salt or sugar dissolves in water, it forms a solution. The water molecules pull the molecules of salt or sugar away from each other and spread them throughout the water. As its molecules disperse in the water, the salt or sugar dissolves in the water and seems to disappear.

Surface tension
The molecules in water have bonds that hold them together. At the surface of the water, the molecules hold each other strongly because there are no molecules pulling on them from above. This strong bond of the surface molecules is called surface tension. It produces an invisible skin over the surface of the water. Surface tension also pulls water drops and bubbles into round shapes.

Water vapour
Water vapour is water in the form of a gas. It forms over the surface of water, and mixes with the air. The vapour is invisible. Air that contains a lot of water vapour is humid. It makes your skin feel damp.

Index

PRINTED IN BELGIUM BY

proost
INTERNATIONAL BOOK PRODUCTION